"Well-behaved women rarely make history."

—Laurel Thatcher Ulrich, American historian

Athena, Greek goddess of handicraft, war, and wisdom

Lives
of Extraordinary
Women

RULERS, REBELS

(and What the Neighbors Thought)

WRITTEN BY KATHLEEN KRULL

ILLUSTRATED BY KATHRYN HEWITT

HARCOURT, INC.

SAN DIEGO   NEW YORK   LONDON

Much gratitude to Jeannette Larson, Queen of Editors, as well as
Diane D'Andrade for her royal influence, Jean Ferris, Susan Cohen,
Sandy Schuckett, Vicky Reed and her extraordinary class at the
University of San Diego, and, as always, Kathryn Hewitt.
—K. K.

Love and praise to glorious Jeannette Larson, Diane Dondratey
(aka Diane D'Andrade), Susan Cohen, Kathleen Krull, Gracie Strauss,
and my extraordinary mother, Mary Moore.
—K. H.

www.harcourt.com

Library of Congress Cataloging-in-Publication Data
Krull, Kathleen.
Lives of extraordinary women: rulers, rebels (and what the neighbors thought)/
written by Kathleen Krull; illustrated by Kathryn Hewitt.
p.   cm.
Includes bibliographical references (p. 95).
[1. Women in politics—Biography—Juvenile literature.   2. Women heads of state—
Biography—Juvenile literature.]   I. Hewitt, Kathryn, ill.   II. Title.
HQ1236.K8   2000
320'.082—dc21   99-6840
ISBN 0-15-200807-1

C E G H F D

Printed in Singapore

The illustrations in this book were done in watercolor and colored pencil on watercolor paper.
The display type was hand lettered by Jane Dill.
The text type was set in Goudy Old Style by R&S Book Composition, La Mesa, California.
Printed and bound by Tien Wah Press, Singapore
This book was printed on totally chlorine-free Nymolla Matte Art paper.
Production supervision by Ginger Boyer
Designed by Linda Lockowitz

For Mariellen Hanrahan, Queen of Minnesota

—K. K.

For three extraordinary women:

Chung Moore, Glenda Davies, and Susan Strauss

—K. H.

Contents

INTRODUCTION • 9

LIFE AT THE LIBRARY
CLEOPATRA • 10

ONE SHOCK AFTER ANOTHER
ELEANOR OF AQUITAINE • 14

A BLAZING LIGHT
JOAN OF ARC • 18

IN THE CHAPEL
ISABELLA I • 22

BEING OUTRAGEOUS
ELIZABETH I • 26

NO FEAR
NZINGHA • 32

EAGLE EYES
CATHERINE THE GREAT • 36

DIAMONDS AND FEATHERS
MARIE ANTOINETTE • 40

SECRETLY AMUSING
VICTORIA • 44

"MOVE OR DIE"
HARRIET TUBMAN • 48

Behind the Curtain
TZ'U-HSI • 52

Dusty for Days
GERTRUDE BELL • 56

"Next Time I'd Be Nastier"
JEANNETTE RANKIN • 60

Lighting a Candle
ELEANOR ROOSEVELT • 64

Strongman or Granny?
GOLDA MEIR • 70

Tiger Among Monkeys
INDIRA GANDHI • 74

Hair Like a Halo
EVA PERÓN • 78

Dancing on the Roof
WILMA MANKILLER • 82

A Splinter of Glass
AUNG SAN SUU KYI • 86

Water Dripping on a Rock
RIGOBERTA MENCHÚ • 90

For Further Reading • 95

Introduction

NOT ALL GOVERNMENTS have been run by men. Here, in chronological order, are twenty women who wielded significant political power, as queens, warriors, prime ministers, revolutionary leaders, Indian chiefs, first ladies, or other government officials.

Each of these extraordinary women triumphed (some at a very young age) over attitudes and conditions that couldn't have been more adverse. Many of the women who are today's beloved heroines were once candidates for "Most Hated Woman on Earth"—and were spat upon, jailed, even murdered. Their electrifying personalities can seem larger than life—but are they really so different from us? What were they like as human beings? What might their neighbors have noticed?

Traditionally, historians have talked most often about what powerful women looked like. This book focuses on daring deeds—and it asks unusually nosy questions, seeking a full picture of these women's lives. Whose secret to success was the library? (Cleopatra.) Who tickled her favorite companion's neck when she thought no one was looking? (Elizabeth I.) Who could raise $50 million in one night, and also did other people's laundry, by hand? (Golda Meir.) Who launched her career at the youngest age? (Joan of Arc, at thirteen.) Who wished she could quit and write novels? (Eleanor Roosevelt.) Who took only two baths in her entire life? (Isabella I.) Whose lips turned green after she nibbled her macaroni necklace? (Eva Perón.)

And who dressed like a man, in animal skins, armed with every possible weapon? (Nzingha.) Who attended séances with her own royal psychic? (Victoria.) Who cut power to the microphones of obnoxious interrupters? (Wilma Mankiller.) Who had three thousand boxes of everyday jewels? (Tz'u-hsi.)

Not all of these women are role models. Like any group of individuals, male or female, this one includes the good, the bad, and some who were both. Their stories are offered here to inspire awe at the power of women throughout history—and ever after.

—Kathleen Krull

Cleopatra

BORN IN 69 B.C. AND DIED IN 30 B.C. IN ALEXANDRIA, EGYPT

*Queen of ancient Egypt, famous for glamorous love affairs,
ambition, and political genius*

WAS CLEOPATRA'S FAMILY *too* close? To keep their power as Egypt's rulers, the Ptolemy family deliberately married one another—sister to brother, parent to child. But some days they weren't close at all. When fighting over the throne, they frequently resorted to murder.

Her father's favorite, Cleopatra spent her childhood in the royal women's apartments. She studied the same subjects as boys, immersing herself in literature, philosophy, the sciences, music, and art. With ambitious relatives and other enemies seething dangerously around her, she developed nerves of steel. At age eighteen she was still alive—and queen. She coped with the required marriage to her ten-year-old brother by pretending he didn't exist. (She was not a good big sister—this brother turned up drowned, and another was poisoned.)

As queen, Cleopatra dedicated herself to keeping Ptolemies in power, with Egypt productive and independent. Above all, she wanted to avoid war with the mighty Roman Empire. The eight languages she spoke came in handy during diplomatic negotiations. She cultivated the good opinion of ordinary Egyptians and conducted the country's business shrewdly.

During her travels, Cleopatra looted foreign libraries for precious papyrus scrolls to add to her world-famous library in Alexandria. She spent much of her time alone there, and it is thought that she may have made her own literary contribution—a volume on cosmetics. With a flair for drama, she constantly experimented with makeup, hairstyles, and new perfumes made from exotic flowers. She bathed in donkey's milk, had servants remove all her unwanted body hair, and soothed her flawless skin with fresh aloe vera leaves.

She did know how to make an entrance. When Julius Caesar, Rome's brilliant military leader, visited Alexandria, he received one of history's most famous gifts: an Oriental carpet—with the queen wrapped inside. (Had she been caught, guards would have killed her on the spot.) Cleopatra and Caesar fell in love instantly; how thrilling that he also happened to be the most powerful ally Egypt could have. Together they cruised the Nile on a royal barge, discussing all the issues of the day, like how best to rule the world. Their son was named Ceasarion.

Romans raised their eyebrows at this power-hungry woman from the mysterious East, a region so strange that it allowed women to rule. Even Caesar's friends grew afraid of her influence (a contributing factor in their successful plot to murder him).

His successor, Marc Anthony, kept sending for Cleopatra. She let time pass, then made another dramatic entrance: She arrived on a ship covered in gold, with sails of purple, and with silver oars rowed in time to flutes and harps that musicians were playing on deck. Anthony won her heart with new scrolls for her library—and by executing her only remaining sibling, a hostile younger sister.

One of history's great love affairs took place in unheard-of luxury. Cleopatra wore pastel robes of filmy silk from remote China, with so many pearl necklaces that it was hard for her to breathe. Banquets showcased the gifts of the Nile—figs, radishes, apricots, peaches. Wine was brought in from Italy at great expense. Anthony and Cleopatra would roast eight boars a night, putting one on the fire every half hour, so that whenever their sophisticated friends were hungry, one boar would always be done just right. Elephant tusks supported tables that displayed jewel-encrusted plates, with forks and spoons made of solid gold. Anthony and Cleopatra spent hours together in the library as well as on the battlefield. They had twins, then a third child.

Romans grew more nervous than ever, and rumors spread that the powerful pair was in danger. Learning that his days were numbered, and believing a false report that Cleopatra was dead, Anthony took his own life. Cleopatra was devastated at the loss of her entertaining companion, and decided to spare Egyptians the sight of their queen being humiliated by the Romans. Determined to make a dramatic exit, she studied ways to die.

According to legend, one night she ate a magnificent meal, had her hairdresser and lady-in-waiting bathe her, and allowed herself to be bitten by a venomous cobra. Her enemies found her dead at age thirty-nine, languishing on a golden couch, oil of cinnamon in her hair, crown perfectly in place.

EVER AFTER

༄ The days of the Ptolemies—and Egyptian independence—were over when Cleopatra died. The Romans executed one of her sons and took her other children to Rome. But the queen of the Nile lived on in the imaginations of those who created poetry, plays (such as Shakespeare's *Antony and Cleopatra*), art, and movies. Two thousand years after her death, she may still be the most famous woman ruler in history.

༄ As the most gossiped-about woman of the ancient world, Cleopatra was so hated that all statues of her were destroyed after her death. Historians of her time called her crazy, evil, arrogant, and much worse. More than a thousand years passed before another woman ruler came to power.

Eleanor of Aquitaine

BORN IN BORDEAUX, AQUITAINE, FRANCE, ABOUT 1122
DIED IN FONTEVRAULT, ANJOU, FRANCE, 1204

*As Queen of France as well as England,
Europe's legendary central figure of the Middle Ages*

YOUNG ELEANOR often accompanied her father, the duke of Aquitaine, as he traveled to castles all over his vast territory. Although he wasn't trying to teach her to rule (women were deemed naturally inferior, even instruments of the devil), Eleanor absorbed his skill as a leader. When he died she was fifteen—and extraordinarily valuable. She had inherited property that was larger than the country of France at that time, could read and write (unlike most women), had unusually sophisticated tastes, and was said to be charming and lively.

The man who became King Louis VII of France was only too happy to marry her, and Eleanor had much influence on him and his country. But she loved to laugh, and life with Louis provided so few opportunities for humor. "I thought to have married a king," she complained, "but find I have wed a monk."

She jumped at the chance to join the Second Crusade, a holy war that would take the couple far from their dull life at home. She offered Louis thousands of her vassals to use as an army and devoted herself to raising money to finance the journey. Shocking society, she gathered three hundred women warriors to accompany her. Along the way, the new sights were dazzling—rare foods, fine fabrics, perfumed water jetting from fountains in Constantinople. But the adventure went badly, and the defeated queen and king returned to France in separate ships.

For a woman to ask for a divorce was unheard of, but Eleanor demanded that Louis release her from her vows; he kept their two children. Now twenty-nine, she was still so valuable that when she rode from his court as fast as she could, she was ambushed by two knights, each intent on claiming her and her land. She escaped and within two months married the most eligible bachelor around, the man who became Henry II of England. Ten years younger than she, he was her equal in ambition. They created an impressive empire by fending off rebels, fortifying borders, and relying on Eleanor's knowledge and experience. She hunted with him for fox and quail, and joined him on long, difficult trips at a moment's notice, crossing the English Channel many times, often while pregnant (she had eight more children). Sometimes she stayed behind to rule in her husband's absence.

Fed up with Henry's many affairs, one day Eleanor simply moved out. She established a court of her own, where poets and musicians thrived, acrobats and jugglers did anything to get laughs, and women ruled. Wearing the finest clothes, in colors to match their moods, the women held mock "courts" of love, in which they handed down verdicts on the behavior of men whose sole purpose was to serve and adore them. It was the birth of the chivalrous tradition and the dawn of a new age for women.

Eleanor dominated her children, and sided with her sons when they tried (unsuccessfully) to overthrow Henry. The rebellion was an act of such startling aggression

that Henry tried to banish Eleanor to a convent. She insisted she was not cut out for a religious life. So he imprisoned her in a remote castle, without money or friends, alone except for guards.

Fifteen long years later, she received news of Henry's death. Within an hour she had been freed and resumed her strenuous life. Wearing red silk gowns trimmed with squirrel fur, jeweled belts showing off her small waist, she traveled constantly from one end of her kingdom to the other. She led armies, introduced financial and legal reforms, worked fiercely to maintain peace, and often risked her life. One of the oldest people alive—and with a good memory—she was trusted by the pope, kings, and emperors.

After sixty-five years as a queen, Eleanor finally went to live at a convent, where she died at age eighty-two.

EVER AFTER

ॐ A dominant political force (her actions continually revised Europe's geography), Eleanor wanted her influence to last. She crafted politically useful marriages for her ten children—several of whom grew up to become kings and queens—and into her eighties was still arranging the marriages of her grandchildren.

ॐ Eleanor changed Europe's idea of what a woman was, and after her death all publicity about her was negative. In his play *King John*, Shakespeare portrayed her as one of his scariest female characters ever. Not until the late 1800s did historians credit her with giving England a big push out of the bleak Middle Ages.

Joan of Arc

BORN IN DOMRÉMY, BARROIS, FRANCE, 1412
DIED IN ROUEN, FRANCE, 1431

*French military heroine and
the model of an inspiring leader*

SHE WAS THIRTEEN when it first happened: She was kneeling in prayer in the garden, where she always was when the noon church bells rang, when a blazing light, brighter than any sunlight, blinded her. She heard her name—Jeanette d'Arc, known to history as Joan of Arc—in the unfamiliar voices of two women and a man. She believed they were saints, telling her that she had been chosen by God to leave her village and save France from the hated English invaders.

Joan began to hear the voices several times a week, and the instructions were increasingly specific. Although Joan burned with desire to go, her stern father had sworn he'd kill any daughter who ran off. So she continued to herd cattle and work in the fields. She did not go to school and never learned to read or write (though later she learned to sign her name). She did not dance, and was known to give up her bed so that a poorer person could sleep there. Though neighbors teased her about being the strictest Catholic around, everyone liked her—except perhaps the man whose marriage proposal she rejected, much to her parents' grief. (He took her to court over it and lost.) She did seem to think of herself as more than a traditional peasant girl; when she was asked why she didn't do more womanly duties, she said, "There are plenty of other women to perform them."

Finally, at age sixteen, she put on her best red dress, cut off her long hair, and left home under cover of night. Through persistence and shrewdness, she managed to convince the French authorities of her mission—and was put in charge of an army. The French had little to lose by giving power to this teenager; the English were already in complete control.

Joan received her own horse, a unique sword with five crosses etched on the blade, and a man's white enameled armor that weighed sixty pounds. She imposed new discipline on the troops (no swearing, looting, or unmarried female companions). Her courage was a blazing inspiration, and soldiers accepted her with little complaint. "Be of good heart!" she urged, always encouraging and eager to proceed into battle. Wounded several times, she'd refuse to leave a battlefield until she was dragged away. She did hate the violence of war and was known to personally console English soldiers as they lay dying. She claimed that she killed only in self-defense. Off the battlefield, for protection, she continued to dress as a man, in leggings and a belted tunic of coarse linen.

It seemed as though Joan had been studying battles for twenty or thirty years. She used military strategies not common until centuries after her lifetime. Her army scored one remarkable victory after another, and Joan became a national heroine.

But in time the tide turned, and one day Joan, fighting wildly, was dragged off her saddle and taken as a prisoner of war. The English jailed her under the tightest security and put her on trial for challenging the authority of the Church—their way of punishing her for trying to overthrow English rule. For five months more than sixty bishops and other clergy questioned, scolded, threatened, and tried to trick her. Denied a lawyer or the right to call witnesses, Joan kept her cool even more heroically than she had on the battlefield. Expertly evading questions day after day, she was sometimes fatigued but never afraid. She was often defiant, giving answers to the effect of "Wouldn't you just like to know?"

Of all the things about Joan that outraged them, the English kept coming back to her men's clothes—considered a crime against the laws of nature. She was sentenced to death and at age nineteen was burned at the stake. Crowds converged to see the "witch-girl" and "cow wench" (an insult to her humble background). Most people jeered and laughed, but even some of her enemies wondered whether the execution was a great mistake.

EVER AFTER

Twenty-two years after Joan's death, France ejected the English forever. Then, at the urging of Joan's mother and many supporters, a second trial was held. This time Joan was quickly cleared of all charges, and the news was celebrated throughout France. Five hundred years later, in 1920, she was canonized as a saint by the Catholic Church.

An estimated ten thousand books have been written about Joan's life, more than about any other woman in history. People have made her a symbol for many different causes, admiring her courage, integrity, and martyrdom in a fight for freedom. Writers inspired by Joan include Shakespeare (who, being English, portrayed her as a fiendish witch in *Henry VI*) and Mark Twain (fascinated with her from the time he was fifteen, he saw her as a valiant heroine).

Isabella I

❧

*Queen of Spain, who made her country
a world power and leader in exploration*

TO AVOID an arranged marriage, Princess Isabella once fled on horseback in the middle of the night. She hated being bullied, and in time she chose to marry Ferdinand of Aragón, who was attractive, athletic, cooperative, and had a ready laugh. He was not as highborn as she was, but she always took his pride into account. She deferred to him in public, saying, "May your Lordship pardon me for speaking of things which I do not understand," even when she spoke of things she understood as well as he did.

But at age twenty-three, when Ferdinand happened to be out of town, she had herself crowned queen. He was stunned, and she appeased him by heralding his return with a grand torchlit procession. As co-rulers they presented a united front even when they didn't agree. She structured the government (making appointments, reorganizing the money system) and administered justice (often with a cruel hand), while his department was war.

Always an indispensable adviser behind the scenes of battle, over time Isabella took an increasingly active role. She scolded Ferdinand and the army for cowardice. She suffered frequent battle hardships, many of which resulted in miscarriages. A genius at organizing supplies, she founded the first military hospital in Europe, sending doctors and medicines into battle with the army. She traveled from town to town to plead for help with her causes, and rode among her troops dressed in magnificent embroidered velvet gowns. Such a hands-on queen was thought quite unnatural. But when she removed her gold-trimmed black hat to reveal her hair shining in the sun, the vision made the troops forget their hardships and fight for her—a saintly figure.

As part of her vision for world expansion, Isabella financed the voyages of Christopher Columbus (Ferdinand agreed reluctantly). The lucky navigator brought back news of the New World, which she promptly made part of Spain. Isabella and Columbus had so much in common that some speculated the relationship was personal, but as a passionate Catholic Isabella was unlikely to have been unfaithful.

She found the strictest priests to be her spiritual advisers. One of them, the legendary Tomás de Torquemada, presided over the Inquisition, a nightmare of paranoia in which thousands of Jews and Muslims were publicly burned to death. Isabella believed it was her duty to "cleanse" her country. Although Spain was united for the first time in eight hundred years, the cost was high. A traveler noticed that "everyone trembled at the name of the queen."

Isabella started meetings at six o'clock in the morning and expected everyone to work as hard as she did (no late parties). She hated bullfighting but enjoyed stalking bears. In her spare time she devoted enormous energy to her five children. She was deeply offended by Ferdinand's many affairs, but also made a place at court for his illegitimate children (at least four). She appeared calm at all times, so concerned with her dignity that during childbirth she requested a veil so the midwife wouldn't see her expression of pain. Off-duty she dressed in simple silk caftans. She reportedly made a spellbinding impression, though it was rumored that (according to custom) she took only two baths in her life.

No one had imagined that she would become queen, so as a child she had spent more time in the chapel than anywhere else, with time out for needlepoint, spinning wool, and gilded painting. She deeply regretted her lack of schooling, forced herself to study Latin and military science when she was middle-aged, and made sure her daughters were brilliantly educated.

The death of her son at age nineteen crushed her; from then on she never let his dog, Bruto, leave her side. When a daughter died soon after, Isabella never fully recovered. She died at age fifty-three.

EVER AFTER

ॐ Isabella left Ferdinand her fabulous collection of jewels—including a famous necklace of gold and pearls with a large ruby—and made every effort to provide for him. In her twenty-eight-page will, addressing every aspect of government, her one personal requirement was that Ferdinand be buried next to her. Gracious as always, she let him choose the site. (Less than two years after her death, he married the eighteen-year-old niece of the French king.)

ॐ Isabella's financing of Columbus's voyages to the New World became her greatest historical achievement, but at the time it was a real gamble. The prospect of unexplored lands full of heathens to convert appealed to her. And if the trips resulted in a new route to the Orient, she wanted Spain to get the credit.

Elizabeth I

BORN IN GREENWICH, ENGLAND, 1533
DIED IN RICHMOND, SURREY, ENGLAND, 1603

❧

*Queen of England and one of the
great rulers of the Western world*

WHEN PRINCESS ELIZABETH was six, it was said, she looked as serious as a forty-year-old. Her most common expression was alarm. King Henry VIII, her father, had beheaded Anne Boleyn, her mother, and Elizabeth grew up subject to the whim of one stepmother after another. Her childhood was one of narrow escapes from imprisonment or worse. Perfecting her technique for giving "answerless answers," she learned to trust no one. When she was eight her father executed another of his wives, and Elizabeth vowed never to marry.

Despite her harrowing childhood, she matured into one of the most educated women of her day, thanks to one of her stepmothers. Scholarship in women was still attacked as evil, but young Elizabeth studied Greek and Roman classics, played music expertly, read history and theology, and became fluent in nine languages. Her tutor marveled that "her mind has no womanly weakness" and thought of her as a freak. Her rare leisure time included horseback rides fast enough to frighten the men who guarded her.

When she was twenty-five, her childhood nightmare ended: She held the power. Many predicted, though, that the reign of Queen Elizabeth would be brief.

Three days into it, she said, "The burden that has fallen on me maketh me amazed." Yet it was her composure that was most amazing. Calm and calculating, she hired capable men as her advisers, issued proclamations, and put a tight lid on government expenses. All her actions, performed with gusto, served her goal of having the English "live in a flourishing and happy condition."

Early in her reign, a delegation of ministers demanded that she marry—without a man by her side, they argued, no woman could function, much less govern a country. Elizabeth's unmarried status was so unusual that it fueled unending speculation and vicious gossip.

The queen forcefully dismissed the delegation. She didn't believe women were equal to men (her ladies-in-waiting were forbidden to talk to her about business). But she was convinced that God meant her to rule, and her gender was no handicap: "I know I have the body of a weak and feeble woman, but I have the heart and stomach of a king."

During her forty-five-year reign as the "Virgin" (unmarried) Queen, the pressure to wed and produce sons never ceased. Every royal bachelor in the world came to woo her. In public she presented herself as "married" to the kingdom, sacrificing personal happiness for the sake of her people. In private she treasured her freedom—she declared, "I will have here but one mistress and no master." She may have also feared childbirth, the most hazardous experience for women at the time. A few times she expressed desire for an heir, but only after she passed childbearing age did she get over her awkwardness around children. Though she was sometimes wistful and lonely, she was more often fiercely independent.

Elizabeth had fun being unmarried, playing games that she always won. She loved receiving proposals, the ritual of courtship, all the flattery and wordplay. She would get engaged for some good political reason, then cancel the wedding at the last minute, skillfully, without hurting feelings—she was always deliciously in control. Her refusal to commit kept all her options open. (Meanwhile, instead of expanding her kingdom through marriage, she simply had her army take countries over.)

At court Elizabeth was a nonstop flirt. She hated men with bad breath, preferred them in fanciful dress (bright silk stockings, velvet high-heeled shoes, and braided beards dyed to match ornate outfits of purple or orange), and loved to watch them dance in leaps and twirls. She had many favorites, particularly her handsome Master of Horse, Robert Dudley. A friend from childhood, he was the man she came closest to marrying. He made her laugh, in loud whoops echoing down the corridors, and she insisted on seeing him at least once a day. During the ceremony promoting him to earl, she reached over and tickled his neck when she thought no one was looking.

Elizabeth kept herself amused by outraging people. Once, when a courtier was bowing to her, she lifted him by his hair. She would stalk out of church if the sermon displeased her. She preferred extremes in entertainment: comedians who provoked uncontrollable giggles, the cruel sport of bearbaiting. Her parties lasted as long as eighteen days, glittering candlelight illuminating the castles, fireworks shaking the walls. She made it known that she liked presents, the more outrageous the better—and she received boxes of rare cinnamon and ginger, a huge chessboard made of marzipan candy, a miniature Saint Paul's Cathedral in sugar paste, eighteen larks in cages, a jeweled bracelet with a tiny clock (the world's first wristwatch).

She could lose her spectacular temper over anything—a card game not going her way, a stuttering speaker, loud noises, beer that wasn't tart enough, reports of injustice, and especially defiance from others. She prided herself on being well informed—"I know more than thou dost," she would snap. Sometimes she got so angry she would faint, and would have to be revived with vinegar. (It was a smelly age, and the queen concocted a pungent fog around herself: vinegar, lemon juice, musk, and rose water.) With her advisers she could be genuinely irresistible, but she could also bully mercilessly, swear, spit, scream personal abuse, and make death threats.

The threats were not always idle. She once slapped a favorite companion during a fight; when he later began a rebellion against her, she had him executed. She also executed (reluctantly) a cousin, Mary, Queen of Scots, for plotting to assassinate her. When two authors wrote an obscene pamphlet about her, she ordered their right hands chopped off. Most notably, she snubbed the Spanish king's offer of marriage, then thoroughly defeated the armada of 130 warships he sent in retaliation—one of the most famous battles in history.

Extraordinarily gracious with her subjects, Elizabeth could make each person think she was addressing him or her alone. "Thank you with all my heart," she would murmur, and she would always make just the right witty remark. In crowds, she never betrayed boredom or hurt feelings.

The entire court, including her staff of 120, traveled constantly between her sixty castles and fifty houses; after a few weeks each place was so unsanitary, it was uninhabitable. She could go to bed at four in the morning, rise at seven, and then require the whole court to do the same. She ate little, though she was always presented with about twenty choices (roast meats, rich sauces, pastries) at her meals. She did like sweets, and eventually lost most of her teeth (which made her speech hard to understand). After dinner she relaxed by rereading favorite passages from the classics or doing a little translation. She adored gossip from around the globe, and wise ambassadors always included "merry tales" in their reports. From her ladies-in-waiting she expected pampering, but they had trouble seeing her as a ruler—this "very strange sort of woman"—without laughing. They played tricks on her and sold information about her private life. Elizabeth fought back, breaking the finger of one, stabbing another in the hand with a fork.

Her women washed her hair in lye and cleaned her teeth with soap and a linen cloth. They decorated her mounds of curls with flowers or jewels—she sparkled when she moved—then laced her into eight layers of clothes and added accessories. Her bulky, elaborate underwear hid her underweight body and amplified her presence, but all the added width made it difficult for her to fit through doorways. In her white makeup (a paste of poisonous lead, egg whites, and poppy seeds that she invented to conceal a bad complexion), she looked like a creature from another world.

More than anything else, Elizabeth adored dancing. One night toward the end of her life she was seen whirling alone in the garden, by the light of the moon. The doctors she distrusted so much predicted she'd kill herself with vigorous walks. But five or six of them died before she did, and she carried on until age sixty-nine.

EVER AFTER

Many historians agree that Elizabeth I was the most successful monarch ever to rule England. When she came to power, the poor, weak island was in danger of being taken over by Spain, but by the time she died, the country was a wealthy force in Europe, with relative peace and a navy that ruled the seas. She sponsored many voyages of discovery, as well as laws and policies that shaped England for centuries to come.

A Protestant, Elizabeth refused to "make windows into men's souls" about religious issues. Her tolerance saved England from the holy wars that devastated other countries. She also eliminated witchcraft trials by insisting that women could not be executed without evidence.

The queen's original poetry, prayers, and speeches reveal more hard work than genius. Yet her love of music, drama, and poetry encouraged enormous cultural growth, and she became the subject of many works of art. With the literary life officially viewed as a worthy endeavor, many of England's greatest writers blossomed, and the earliest women writers referred to Elizabeth as a scholar whose work made their own possible.

N o   F e a r

Nzingha

BORN ABOUT 1580 AND DIED IN 1663 IN
PORTUGUESE WEST AFRICA, NOW CALLED ANGOLA

*West African queen, ruler of present-day Angola,
famous for resistance to slave traders*

NZINGHA HARBORED fiery ambition and vision, but she also needed patience. One of five children of the king of Ndongo, part of central West Africa, she endured decades of violent invasion by Portuguese traders in human flesh.

Some historians report that Nzingha's brother took the throne, then killed her son, and that she later poisoned her brother in revenge. Rumor had her also murdering her nephew—and eating his heart. Whatever the truth, she benefited from both deaths and grabbed power for herself, becoming ruler of the kingdom at age forty-two. Forbidding her subjects to call her queen, Nzingha took the title of king and promptly launched a war to regain her country's independence.

She proved to be the invaders' worst nightmare. She could be diplomatic, barbaric . . . whatever worked. She found resourceful ways to add to her army, like freeing any slave who escaped to her land and making him a soldier instead. She ordered troops to pretend to be captured by the Portuguese, then steal all the firearms they could and return to her. She worked with other Europeans, notably the Dutch, to form alliances that increased her strength, and gained respect even from those who considered Africans subhuman. To suit her purposes, she once dragged out negotiations for a peace treaty for eight years. She used religion as a political tool and went along with the Portuguese desire to baptize her, taking the Christian name of Anna. Later she

33

renounced Christianity, and to gain the respect of the fiercest tribe around, she adopted cannibalism.

Nzingha was at her most ruthless in combat. She simply had no fear. Personally leading her forces into the heat of battle, she was as nimble as her much younger warriors, and she would rally her forces by striking two iron bells. Making the scariest of impressions, she dressed as a man—cloaking herself with the skins of wild animals, and arming herself with sword, ax, and bow and arrows. She lured her enemies farther and farther inland, gaining the advantage. She was always being cornered—and always making miraculous escapes. She never hurt the prisoners she took, and commanded her servants and soldiers not to, either.

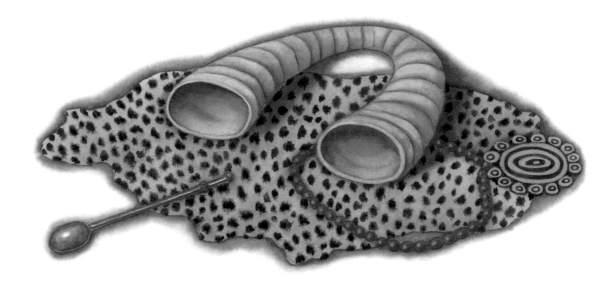

Enemies despised her for her race, sex, and relatively old age. According to the best-known legend about her, she attended a peace conference with the Portuguese, preceded by her musicians and a horde of servants. The men assumed they had the upper hand—and they did have all the chairs. Nzingha shrewdly recognized the "oversight" as an insult and turned to her attendants. One came forward immediately and dropped to hands and knees. The queen lightly sat upon her servant's back, and with this one elegant gesture showed who was in charge. Flabbergasted by her nerve, the Portuguese signed a peace treaty on the spot.

Nzingha never married, but kept fifty or sixty young men as bodyguards. She made her favorites wear women's clothes and allowed them to move freely among the women of her household. If any displeased her, he was not seen again.

She appointed women to the highest government positions and especially promoted her sisters, Mukumbu and Kifunji. When the Portuguese captured one sister, Nzingha later traded 130 slaves for her release. Another sister was also taken prisoner, and kept the queen supplied with secret information for years, until the Portuguese drowned her.

Dominating the politics of the entire region for forty years, Nzingha fought on until her death at the then-amazing age of eighty-two. Her corpse was put on formal display, dressed in royal robes encrusted with jewels, a bow and arrow clasped in her hand.

EVER AFTER

Though her struggle helped awaken others around her, no strong ruler followed Nzingha. The Portuguese prevailed, and this area of West Africa suffered more lasting damage from the slave trade than any other. Not until 1975 did Angola become independent of Portugal. Today, Nzingha is hailed as a patriotic heroine in the People's Republic of Angola, her life the basis for many oral stories throughout Africa.

As a symbol of national resistance against overwhelming odds, Nzingha has inspired people in many places. In America in the 1800s, early abolitionists used her to argue with those who thought blacks were naturally inferior. One antislavery writer noted, "History furnishes very few instances of bravery, intelligence, and perseverance equal to the famous Nzingha, the Negro queen of Angola."

Catherine the Great

BORN IN SZCZECIN, POLAND, 1729
DIED NEAR SAINT PETERSBURG, RUSSIA, 1796

❧

Russian empress for thirty-four years,
during which Russia became a world power

WHEN CATHERINE SEIZED the Russian throne at age thirty-three, she had absolutely no right to it. She wasn't even Russian (though it was rumored that she'd asked her doctor to drain her blood and replace it with that of a Russian). She was a German princess who had been brought to Russia to marry Peter, the future emperor. She spent the next eighteen years with one of the world's least appealing husbands; Peter heaped abuse on her, tortured their dogs, emptied his wine over the heads of his footmen, and brought his toy soldiers to bed, forcing her to participate in mock military maneuvers. Catherine held on by immersing herself in literature and riding her horse some thirteen hours a day, saying, "The more violent the exercise was, the more I loved it."

Unpopular with everyone, Peter was overthrown six months into his reign; with the support of the Imperial Guard, Catherine was crowned empress. Six days later Peter died mysteriously, and she plunged into the work of sorting out Russia's chaos.

She wrote guidelines for a new code of laws, reduced religious persecution, tripled the number of factories, and embarked on mapping her vast territory and assembling the country's first dictionary. She reorganized the army and navy, appeared in battles, and aggressively enlarged Russia's boundaries, doubling its population. She founded Russia's first medical school and, with great pomp, set an example by getting a shot to prevent smallpox, which was the most deadly disease among children.

Passionate about improving education in her mostly illiterate empire—there were no teachers, no textbooks—Catherine sponsored the *General Plan for the Education of Young People of Both Sexes*. (Ignored by her parents because she wasn't a boy, she had been well educated by a French governess.) She founded the first school for girls and personally paid the tuition for those without money. In a society where women had few rights (a man could legally cut off his wife's nose if she offended him), Catherine made the first efforts at bettering their lives and appointed some women to important posts.

Though she was barely five feet tall, she awed visitors: "The head held high, the eagle eyes, the assured bearing that comes with the habit of command... so majestic that she seemed to rule the world." She took plots against her life very seriously and sentenced the guilty to hard labor in Siberia. But she did love to laugh, and her fond servants stayed with her for years.

"Useful" was Catherine's motto, and everything else in life was incidental to power. She woke up early, lit a fire, drank strong black coffee, rubbed her face with an ice cube, and wrote for several hours. (She felt compelled to fill blank paper, and she poured her heart into letters and lengthy memoirs. She also wrote operas, essays on history, and the first stories for children ever published in Russia.) Two meals a day were enough, and Catherine didn't care if the menu was boiled beef over and over. She retired early each night, with her current companion.

With utter disregard for society's standards, Catherine had some twelve to twenty companions, usually intellectual younger men, each relationship lasting from two to twelve years. She enjoyed educating the men politically, and gave each one a palace when she was ready to move on. She refused to remarry, and had three sons with different fathers. A doting grandmother, she took full charge of her grandsons' education.

A self-professed "glutton for beauty," she collected thousands of the finest paintings rubles could buy, founded an art academy, built extravagant palaces complete with roller coasters on the lawn, and imported a frog-themed dinner service of nine hundred pieces.

Leaving Russia much stronger, more prosperous, and more beautiful than she had found it, she was discovered dead in her bathroom by her maid, having suffered a stroke at age sixty-seven.

EVER AFTER

Catherine hated the brutal system of serfdom (under which more than half the population lived in appalling conditions), and she tried various ways to dismantle it. Unwilling to use force, however, she also dreaded alienating the nobility, who depended on the labor of the serfs for their great estates. Increasingly tyrannical toward the end of her life, she may have made the situation worse, and her actions led indirectly to the Russian Revolution of 1917.

Catherine's hold on the throne was not strong enough for her to do all she wished, and her contributions were overlooked for years. She was notorious instead for exaggerated rumors about her social life. With communism's collapse in the twentieth century, scholars began to focus on Catherine and others who played key roles in shaping modern Russia.

Catherine's magnificent palace at Peterhof, outside Saint Petersburg, is now Russia's most popular tourist attraction, drawing six million visitors each year.

Marie Antoinette

BORN IN VIENNA, AUSTRIA, 1755
DIED IN PARIS, FRANCE, 1793

જ

*Queen of France for almost twenty years
and a major catalyst of the French Revolution*

AS THE FAVORITE DAUGHTER of formidable empress Maria Theresa of Austria, Marie Antoinette was taught little else besides music and how to please (her most important duty). At age fourteen, her tears falling on velvet pillows, she was shipped off to France to marry the future King Louis XVI. When she became queen at age nineteen, she knew she was out of her depth: "I was too young and thoughtless."

Peasants liked her at first—she supported charities, helped children in school, and allowed the people to roam the royal lands. Whenever peasants were accidentally trampled or shot during Louis's hunting trips, Marie always stopped to help nurse the injured. She was also generous with the nine hundred servants at her lavish palace of Versailles.

The corrupt, highly judgmental nobles resented her at once. To break the tension, she would flick bread crumbs across the dinner table and poke fun at older women's wrinkles—and would then make enemies simply by laughing with her mouth open. ("How gauche!" sneered the nobles.) People who stood in the courtyard could get pails of waste dumped on their heads—and somehow it kept happening to Marie. Never intentionally cruel, she was always amazed when she wasn't liked. "Why should they hate me? What have I ever done to them?" she would wail.

Desperate for affection and sympathy, requiring orange-flower water to revive her from fainting fits, she masked anxiety with gaiety. Louis wanted her to keep the court entertained, as did all those who believed women should be steered clear of politics. So each night, by the light of hundreds of chandeliers, the best of French society enjoyed the finest food and wine and the wittiest talk. When Marie returned to her shockingly messy rooms at the palace, she allowed her beloved pug dogs to tear holes in the tapestries and chew on the gilded chairs. When she wasn't gambling the nights away, she went to the quaint peasant village she designed as a retreat for herself; there she milked her two cows, Brunette and Blanchette, and spent hours alone. Her amusements provided jobs for thousands of people. She considered their employment her political duty, and urged the dismissal of ministers who disapproved.

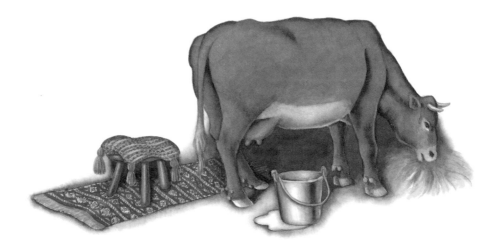

A visitor described Marie as "glittering like the morning star, full of life and splendor and joy." A glamorous risk taker, she increasingly set the cultural style in France, and her influence spread throughout Europe. She supported the most gifted craftsmen and while walking to Mass every day would acknowledge the artists and writers in the crowd, each nod or smile indicating her current favorites. Twice a year she ordered thirty-six new gowns and countless accessories in shades of purple (when others were wearing brownish tones known as "flea's stomach," "Paris mud," or "indiscreet tears").

She also set trends in hair, combing hers upward over large cushions topped with fruit or figurines. She was so passionate about feathered headdresses, cresting two or three feet high, that critics labeled her "featherhead." Everyone believed the false report that she'd purchased the most expensive necklace in the world, a collar of 540 diamonds.

Marie wasn't taken seriously until she had a son, after eleven years as queen. Then she accepted responsibility by reading more, forcing her weak husband (whose main interest was designing new locks and other odd repair jobs around the palace) to stand up to corrupt ministers, often confronting them herself. When peasants, furious about their terrible living conditions, mobbed the palace, she faced them with such bravery that some lowered their guns. As massacres began, she endlessly plotted escape (always including her children in the plan). But in a humiliating trial, she was charged with absurd offenses and condemned to death.

Just thirty-seven but already ghostlike, Marie was slowly driven around Paris for three hours, while crowds jeered and spat at her. Mounting the steps of the guillotine, wearing her purple slippers, she apologized for accidentally stepping on the executioner's foot. All witnesses agreed that she was calm and showed no fear.

Ever After

After her execution Marie's eight-year-old son was placed in solitary confinement and died within two years. Her daughter, imprisoned until age sixteen, married a cousin and lived another fifty unhappy years. Meanwhile, the French Revolution took thousands of lives and changed the course of world history.

Marie Antoinette was probably one of the most hated women of all time, her name a synonym for royal selfishness. Although she was not the cause of France's serious troubles, she was the most visible scapegoat. She may have had one affair (with a Swedish noble), but gossip flowed that she had many, and "fat pig" was the nicest description of her in the degrading propaganda of the day. Yet she almost certainly didn't say her most famous words ("Let them eat cake!" in response to a famine), and the mass hysteria may have been due to her position—the fear of women in power has even been termed the Marie Antoinette syndrome.

SECRETLY AMUSING

Victoria

BORN IN LONDON, ENGLAND, 1819
DIED ON ISLE OF WIGHT, ENGLAND, 1901

*Queen of England for sixty-four years,
the longest royal lifetime in history*

VICTORIA'S FIRST ACT as queen, at age eighteen, was to move her bed out of her domineering mother's room. A miserable childhood had toughened her. After she inherited the throne, she became extremely wealthy (with 445 servants to manage, most of whom revered her), and free to display her iron will in an era when women were supposed to appear delicate. (Many women put leeches behind their ears to drain the blood and whiten their cheeks.)

"We are not amused," she once said after a guest told a racy story at dinner; her words plunged the room into dead silence. Though respectable and prim in public (like the Victorian age named for her), she could be witty and down-to-earth in private. She had a silvery chuckle and could laugh until she cried, her whole body shaking.

On the job, Victoria blossomed. "The Queen will not be dictated to," she said to anyone who tried, sweeping all the objects off her desk or stamping her feet for effect. "I *delight* in this work!" she wrote in the secret diary she kept all her life. She commanded respect, even from those who judged her by appearance ("a more homely little being you never beheld").

She delayed marriage because she dreaded the possibility of no longer getting her own way, but eventually wed Albert, a penniless German prince. "He is *perfection*," she wrote, raving about his "exquisite" beauty. They worked at adjoining desks, lit by a green-shaded reading lamp. Every morning, no matter how early she began work, she would find a neat stack of papers he had reviewed and arranged for her inspection. Above all, he kept her amused—and was her best friend.

Conscientious about each of her duties, the queen provided nine heirs to the throne. Each night her children came before her one by one, so she could quiz them and do her best to manipulate their behavior. Her grandchildren were more apt to remember her for hugs, peppermints, and the circuses she brought to the palace.

Victoria relaxed at Balmoral, the seventy-room retreat she bought (fleeing London after seven attempts on her life) in the remote Highlands of Scotland. She loved hiking through the wild countryside, muddying her boots and pausing to draw detailed sketches. At night she read novels (Jane Austen was a favorite author), or sat at her spinning wheel while someone read poetry to her, a plate of pralines and fondant cookies and a glass of whiskey nearby. She loved food, the richer the better, and she ate it fast and often. Playing solitaire was a treat, but only if she won.

She cultivated her domestic side by embroidering vests for Albert and sewing a quilt for each grandchild. Her closets overflowed with satin gowns and dainty accessories. She was somewhat old-fashioned, and preferred candlelight to electricity, writing by hand to the typewriter, and the traditional paper square instead of the new toilet-paper rolls. A Protestant, she was tolerant of other religions, and she found racism intolerable.

Albert did have at least one flaw—he was not strong physically—and he died after catching a cold while scolding their oldest son in the rain. The shock overwhelmed Victoria, a widow at forty-two, and she never entirely forgave her son. She preserved every detail of Albert's room, kept a plaster cast of his hand in her bed, and wore his picture on a chain around her neck (often holding it up so he could "see"). She began to dabble in the occult, holding séances and appointing her own royal psychic. Inspiring oceans of gossip about a secret marriage, she became close to John Brown, Albert's handsome Scottish servant, to help her feel near the spirit of her husband. The queen took years to resume her public duties.

Eventually regaining her toughness (and finding things amusing again), Victoria sailed on for another forty years as her country became the most powerful in the world. Until a few days before she died, at age eighty-two, after a stroke, she was conducting business.

Ever After

⤷ One of Victoria's preoccupations was finding suitable mates for her children, grandchildren, and thirty-seven great-grandchildren. Marrying them into every royal family in Europe freed her reign of virtually all threats of war. Most members of today's European monarchies are related to Victoria.

⤷ "I consider my vocation to be that of trying to do good in the world," Victoria wrote. Yet her policies poisoned England's relations with Ireland, and she failed to help those who suffered through the Industrial Revolution—thirty thousand children lived on London's streets. She was violently opposed to giving women the vote. Feminists, she claimed, "ought to get a good whipping," and women were deemed "not fitted to reign"—she put on a show of disliking her duty. (Ironically, her very public role as a working mother strengthened the women's rights movement.)

⤷ Committed to expanding England into an empire on which the sun never set, she took over a quarter of the globe. Places all over—in Texas, Canada, Antarctica, Africa—have been named after her. Victoria's name even graces a chain of stores that sell underwear.

Harriet Tubman

BORN NEAR BUCKSTOWN, MARYLAND, ABOUT 1820
DIED IN AUBURN, NEW YORK, 1913

❧

American leader during the Civil War era,
known as the queen of the Underground Railroad

"I THINK SLAVERY is the next thing to hell," Harriet Tubman said. Her parents had been taken from the Ashanti tribe, warriors of West Africa, and brought to America as slaves; they had eleven children. At age five Harriet was put to work as a housekeeper and baby-sitter, and she grew up in fear. The scars on her back from many whippings were permanent, as was the brain damage after a two-pound lead weight was thrown at her head. (She was prone to violent headaches and sudden blackouts.)

As a teen she much preferred working in the fields to indoor work—splitting fence rails, loading timber on wagons, checking muskrat traps. She was small, but had mighty muscles and fierce eyes. Her father taught her how to survive in the perilous woods around them—how to use the North Star as a compass, which wild berries and fruit were edible.

Her husband, John Tubman, threatened to betray her if she tried to escape slavery. The risk of capture was crushing, and no escaped slave had ever returned—death was certain. But a white neighbor told Harriet about the Underground Railroad, a secret network of free blacks and white sympathizers who helped runaways escape to freedom in the North. At age twenty-nine, she decided to try.

Late one night, telling no one, Tubman packed her patchwork quilt (all the more precious because she had hated the "indoor" work of sewing it), some corn bread, and

49

some salted herring. She hitched a ride to the first of her many stops along the ninety miles from the plantation to Philadelphia, so overcome by gratitude that she gave the wagon driver her quilt.

"I was a stranger in a strange land," Tubman said later. She went to work in a hotel kitchen and hoarded her money. Soon neighbors noticed that she was often absent for weeks at a time. She was doing the unthinkable—going back into slave territory and guiding others to freedom. She first helped her family, then ultimately more than three hundred other people, during a total of nineteen trips. After her husband refused to join her, she rarely spoke of him again.

Tubman's sheer guts stood out to everyone who knew her. "I can't die but once" was her motto. She was a genius at planning every detail of a journey, from food and shelter to sleeping pills for crying babies. She knew every route through treacherous swamps and forests, on the darkest nights groping her way from tree to tree. Trading knowledge with other Underground Railroad leaders, she took great pride in her work and had a wry sense of humor. She wore men's suits (better for travel than long, full skirts) and carried a gun.

On her most famous trip, she pointed her gun at the head of a panicky man who wanted to turn back. "Move or die," she ordered, knowing that he could be tortured into giving the others away. Her heroic exploits and narrow escapes made her a legend among slaves, while Southern plantation owners (assuming a woman would be incapable of such daring) offered the tremendous sum of $40,000 for "his" capture.

Feeling like "a blackberry in a pail of milk," Tubman began speaking publicly, helping whites understand why slavery was immoral. Her audiences would rush to shake the hand of this unpretentious, neatly dressed woman who was missing many teeth. She never learned to read or write, but had memorized much of the Bible and spoke eloquently, with a biblical rhythm.

Tubman's knowledge of the terrain proved valuable to the Union army when the Civil War broke out. She served for more than three years as spy, nurse, and the only woman to lead troops into battle, receiving numerous commendations. After the war she married Nelson Davis, a handsome veteran twenty-four years her junior.

Later in life, in a two-story redbrick home in New York, she planted a large vegetable garden and took in orphans and the elderly. Over hot tea with butter, she recounted her adventures to whoever knocked on her door.

Tubman's last cause was women's rights. "Tell the women to stand together," she said, a month before she died of pneumonia, at ninety-three.

EVER AFTER

Though many slaves fought back, most Americans of the time, black and white, took slavery for granted. One of the most daring leaders in history, Tubman was one of the few whose resistance was both dramatic and effective. By enraging Southerners, she contributed to the conflicts between the North and South that gave rise to the Civil War and led to slavery's abolition.

Queen Victoria awarded Tubman a silver medal and sent a letter that Tubman nearly wore out looking at. Meanwhile, the U.S. government eventually granted her a tiny pension—not for her own work, but as the widow of a veteran. The profits of a book by a neighbor, called *Scenes in the Life of Harriet Tubman*, were a help (though the book's introduction apologized for trying "to make a heroine of a black woman").

In 1998, urging contributions for the restoration of Tubman's last home in Auburn, Hillary Rodham Clinton called her "a symbol of the enduring spirit of this nation. We should be hearing the voice of Harriet Tubman in our ears."

Tz'u-hsi

❧

Empress of China, ruler of one-third the world's
population during forty-seven years of great change

CHINESE SOCIETY was structured to keep women virtual slaves, yet a few throughout history achieved power—and Tz'u-hsi was the most memorable. Clever, beautiful girls could become companions to royal men, and fourteen-year-old Tz'u-hsi went willingly when her family nominated her as one. Life inside the Forbidden City, a vast complex of palaces surrounded by pink walls thirty-five feet high, was a haven from parts of China where women were still being crippled by having their feet bound.

Tz'u-hsi was not taught to read or write, but to arrange flowers, play music, be obedient and perfectly groomed (a red dot was painted on her lower lip), and prepare for childbearing. Companions were not supposed to meddle in political affairs, but Emperor Hsien Feng did trust Tz'u-hsi's judgment and was said to consult her. At age twenty-one, she became the only one of his wives and companions to give birth to a son—and thus gained enormous power literally overnight. When the emperor died, Tz'u-hsi seized control as the mother of the new (five-year-old) emperor. At meetings that began at four o'clock in the morning, her son sat in her lap, while she handed down decisions from behind a gauze curtain, to give the illusion of invisibility required for women.

Servants carried the empress to meetings in a shrouded chair, after hours of preparing her appearance. A vault held three thousand ebony boxes of "everyday jewels," most received as gifts; to display as many as possible, Tz'u-hsi changed clothes and accessories many times a day. She preferred phoenixes, rather than the traditional imperial dragons, embroidered on her silk gowns. She wore fresh flowers in her elaborately braided hair, musk perfume, and jeweled protectors over her three-inch fingernails.

Tz'u-hsi's survival required virtue (she would have been immediately executed otherwise), boldness (she broke traditions constantly), and expert manipulation of those around her. She reacted aggressively when threatened, once saying dryly, "As has always been the case in emergencies, I was equal to the occasion." She brought in scholars to tutor her and became well educated. No man was allowed to sit in her presence (a problem when cars came into use, as no chauffeur could sit down near her). As a woman she was not permitted to meet a foreigner (but she did at age sixty-three), nor to travel outside the Forbidden City (which she did at age seventy).

A visitor said he had never seen more "tremendous will power" in a human being—nor as much "kindness and love." Tz'u-hsi seemed anxious to be liked, patting women on the cheek and handing over jade statues that anyone admired. But she laughed only when she played with her Pekingese dogs (each wore a bright ribbon secured with a pearl clip, and they had their own palace with marble floors). She hated cats, and none of her three thousand servants was allowed to keep one. Her favorite number was six; she ordered all furniture to be made in sixes. She was skilled at painting and, when worried, would call for her brushes and ink. Her red lacquered chests held huge collections of mechanical toys.

After a breakfast of warm lotus-root porridge, Tz'u-hsi would walk on intricate paths among blossoming peach, plum, and cherry trees, crossing bridges over ponds full of golden carp. Snacks were pine nuts and honeysuckle tea. For dinner, at the sound of a gong, she would enter a chamber and choose from 150 dishes—from eggs poached in chicken broth (her favorite) and pork with cherries, to bear's paw stuffed with mushrooms and the laboriously prepared Peking duck.

Despite her attempts to retire, national turmoil kept the empress in power until age seventy-three, when she appointed Pu Yi, her nephew's nephew, as her successor. She soon had a stroke, and died two days later. Her feelings about her role were mixed. Her final words were "Never again allow a woman to hold the supreme power in the State."

Ever After

꧁ Tz'u-hsi had struggled to keep her Manchu dynasty from unraveling, and after she died it lasted just three more years. The last emperor, Pu Yi, was forced to step down, and he spent the rest of his life as an ordinary citizen of Communist China.

꧁ Few rulers have received such bad press as Tz'u-hsi has. It took the *New York Times* six weeks to assemble its obituary, which referred to her by another woman's name, and used a photo of yet another woman. Chinese and Western historians have portrayed her as an evil tyrant with a disgusting lifestyle. Only in recent years has a truer picture emerged, but even today the People's Republic of China uses her as a symbol of hated imperialism—in movies Tz'u-hsi is portrayed as a ruler who beheads people, saws them into pieces, and hurls them down wells.

Gertrude Bell

BORN IN DURHAM, ENGLAND, 1868
DIED IN BAGHDAD, IRAQ, 1926

British government official known as the "Uncrowned Queen of Iraq"

LIKE OTHER privileged girls, young Gertrude Bell required a chaperone to accompany her on the street, parental approval to read books or visit people, and constant grooming for her anticipated wedding.

Despite several close calls, no wedding took place. Instead, Bell became one of the first women at Oxford University, earning a degree in modern history, and then venturing further and further from home. She fell in love with sand: To her, the Middle East was paradise, its desolation broken by groves of date palms, glowing wildflowers, two-foot-long lizards, and the corpses of travelers who hadn't survived the harsh desert sun.

When exploring remote archaeological sites, she could cross the desert with just two tents and a month's supplies. She could also travel in a caravan of twenty camels and trunks filled with crystal goblets, volumes of Shakespeare, a tea service, and a canvas bathtub for hot soaks at night. To fool officials who might search her possessions, she buried revolvers in a trunk of frilly underwear. Once, a dozen thieves surrounded Bell's group, shrieking and brandishing swords before making off with weapons and coats. Another time she was kidnapped by a desert warrior and held prisoner for two weeks.

Bell's best skill, luckily, was talking. "English women are never afraid," she said, and many people assumed she was some sort of queen. She could switch from language to language (she mastered at least seven) and from frivolous gossip to intense negotiation, always gathering more information than she revealed. In Arab camps it never occurred to her to use the women's quarters (and she absolutely refused to wear a veil like Arab women). She sat cross-legged in the men's tents, puffing on Egyptian cigarettes, sipping thick Turkish coffee. Like her hosts, she ate meat with her hands, using flat bread to scoop up yogurt, and she never flinched at the sheep's eyes served to her as honored guest.

She was not a testy traveler (even when coated with dust for days at a time), unless her clothes failed to arrive. High atop a camel, she wore simple, divided skirts and a man's khaki jacket. Off the camel, she delighted in hats topped with peaches or cherries, stylish evening gowns of purple chiffon trimmed with ostrich feathers, brocade slippers, and lavish fur coats or fringed shawls.

With her unusual understanding of the area, Bell was uniquely qualified to work as a British spy during World War I. She turned her explorations into vital reports, and many considered her the most powerful woman in the British Empire of her day. In 1918, on a piece of tracing paper, Bell drew the boundaries for a new country called Iraq. She helped choose its first ruler, Prince (later King) Faisal, and was his closest adviser.

In her spare time she climbed mountains, went horseback riding (taking her Arab greyhounds, Rishan and Najmah), wrote thousands of letters to her parents (some fifteen pages long), kept detailed diaries, published popular books, and took more than seven thousand archaeologically valuable photographs. She was active in the anti-suffragist movement—while she believed herself equal to any man, she thought most other women were not, and for them to vote could be dangerous. She pitied Arab women for their constrained lives, and fought to establish schools for girls.

An atheist, Bell believed most ardently in Great Britain as the savior of the world. But she rarely went back to her homeland, saying, "I have seen strange things, and they color the mind." Her nieces and nephews found her tart and imperious, as did some men—one ridiculed her as a "conceited, gushing, flat-chested man-woman."

Bell mourned that her "wild travel" seemed incompatible with marriage. "What I really want is a wife," she wrote, frustrated by her lack of companionship. Increasingly lonely and depressed as Iraq became more independent and needed her less, she died from an overdose of sleeping pills at age fifty-seven.

EVER AFTER

꿍 "We are making history," Bell told King Faisal. But when he died, in 1933, Iraq became unstable; after a series of military takeovers, president Saddam Hussein took control in 1979. Bell was all but forgotten until late in the twentieth century. During the Persian Gulf War in 1991, disputes over Iraq's borders were traced back to her actions.

꿍 Unlike many of her British colleagues, Bell had great esteem for Middle Eastern culture. In shaping the terms of Iraq's independence from Great Britain (and ensuring her home country an oil-rich stake in the area), she envisioned Iraq as "a center of Arab civilization and prosperity."

꿍 So far, no movie has been made about Bell's life, but *Lawrence of Arabia* is about legendary British hero T. E. Lawrence, her much more famous friend and protégé. (She called him "you little imp.")

"Next Time I'd Be Nastier"
Jeannette Rankin

BORN NEAR MISSOULA, MONTANA, 1880
DIED IN CARMEL, CALIFORNIA, 1973

First woman elected to the U.S. Congress

"IT MAKES NO DIFFERENCE where," Jeannette Rankin wrote in her diary, "just so you go! go! go!" But where *would* she go? She showed promise in architecture and furniture design, careers that weren't open to women at the time. She graduated from the brand-new University of Montana with a degree in biology and worked as a teacher, seamstress, and social worker. She had several proposals, but—having grown up with much responsibility for rearing her six younger siblings—she thought marriage would mean giving up her freedom.

At age thirty, she began to fight to get Montana women the right to vote. (When one politician threw a glass of water in her face, she swore that women would someday throw him out of office.) Four years later, the fight having been successful, Rankin decided to try for a seat in the U.S. Congress.

Most people thought she had no chance. Her sisters left home to work for her campaign, and her wealthy brother Wellington served as her manager and trusted adviser. The day after she defeated seven men in the election, newspaper photographers mobbed her house, wanting to know if she was a freak, what she looked like, if she could cook.

In Washington, petty problems included the lack of women's bathrooms in the Capitol, plus fear from the wives of congressmen (one was relieved to find Rankin "just a sensible young woman going about her business"). Whenever possible, Rankin sat next to the oldest, most white-haired man around, to avoid flirtation or harassment. Her sixth day on the job, she became one of the fifty-six unpopular members of Congress who voted against entering World War I. She fully supported the United States once it did declare war, but she lost her next two elections.

"I felt," she insisted later, "that the first time the first woman had a chance to say no to war, she should say it." She had finally found her "where"—pacifism. For the next twenty years, Rankin worked day and night for world peace. She saw war as a tragic waste: "You can no more win a war than you can win an earthquake."

Nearing age sixty, she set out to face "the cold, stupid world" by running for Congress once again—and winning. Soon President Franklin Roosevelt asked Congress to declare war on Japan. The vote was 388 to 1.

"As a woman I can't go to war," said Rankin, "and I refuse to send someone else." She was serene and confident, but the crowd burst into boos. In the madness of flashbulbs and the crush of angry people against her, she slipped into a phone booth and called police to escort her back to her office. She was instantly notorious as the only person to vote against both World Wars. No one supported her (even Wellington was stunned), and once she finished her term her public political career was over.

Rankin returned to lecturing on world peace. Between her many trips to India (she became obsessed with the work of pacifist Mohandas Gandhi), she lived as cheaply as

possible in rural Georgia, with a dachshund named Sam. Famous for her lemon meringue pie, she befriended children from the neighborhood, seeking their opinions, sharing stories of her life.

In Washington, in 1967, at eighty-seven years old, she led a silent march of five thousand women dressed in black—and brought national attention to the fact that not *everyone* supported the Vietnam War. She hired a motorcycle-riding young man as her assistant; he cooked health foods (she drank raw eggs) and worked at keeping her in the public eye. She was even tempted to try for a third congressional term, but her health failed and she died peacefully at age ninety-two.

She once hinted that the penalty for her years of protest had been steep: "Look at me—unmarried and unemployed most of my life!" But when asked how she'd live life differently, she said she'd do everything the same—only "this time I'd be nastier."

Ever After

⌒ Injecting a new voice into national political debates, Rankin always promoted legislation benefiting women, addressing numerous problems previously considered unmentionable. Her biggest triumph was to introduce the Nineteenth Amendment in Congress, and seeing it ratified in 1920, after a long fight. "If I am remembered for no other act, I want to be remembered as the only woman who ever voted to give women the right to vote," she said.

⌒ When she spoke in high schools, Rankin predicted a woman president someday soon. Boys would burst into laughter, then fall silent when she reassured them that there would be "opportunities for boys, too. Someday one of you may be the husband of a president." She also pushed for women's equal representation in Congress, but in 1998 women made up just eleven percent of the group (though they do now have their own bathrooms).

Eleanor Roosevelt

BORN IN 1884 AND DIED IN 1962 IN NEW YORK CITY

*Powerful American first lady and one of
the world's foremost champions for human rights*

AS A CHILD, Eleanor Roosevelt was afraid of the dark, water, mice, pain, disappointing people, failure, and much else. She was an orphan by age eight, starved for affection and praise. Nearly everyone called her ugly. Her grandmother sent her, at age fifteen, to finishing school in England, and there she blossomed in her study of languages and literature. Her secret desire was to write novels or plays. She began volunteering in needy communities, her fear ebbing into compassion. And of Franklin, her fearless fifth cousin, whom she married, she said, "I have never known a man who gave one a greater sense of security."

The night he was elected president of the United States, someone discovered Eleanor crying alone—"Now I'll have no identity," she mourned. Almost immediately, however, she realized that her marriage to the most powerful man in the world did have advantages. Years earlier, after discovering a packet of love letters that revealed Franklin's affair with her secretary, she chose not to divorce him (which would have ruined his political career), but rather to somehow forge a career of her own. Now she became a major adviser to Franklin during his twelve troubled years in office, when crises included the Great Depression and World War II.

Previously ignored groups soon had a voice in the White House—African Americans, women, the poor, young people. Roosevelt marched into muddy fields to inspect migrant workers' living conditions, descended into coal mines to interview miners, fought (unsuccessfully) to allow more European Jewish refugees into the United States, and traveled as many as twenty-three thousand miles a year to encourage American servicemen. During wartime hysteria, she urged fair treatment of Japanese Americans (newspapers responded by urging her removal from public life). Her talk was peppered with "Franklin, I think you should...," and "Franklin, surely you will not..." She sometimes removed insulting COLORED ONLY signs; when whites complained, Franklin would say, "Well, it's my missus and I can't control her." She'd arrange the seats at dinner parties to put him next to authors who promoted her favorite causes. She pushed papers in his face so often during meals that a daughter once said, "Mother, can't you see you are giving Father indigestion?"

Roosevelt liked to get places fast, and was the first American president's wife to travel by plane and to drive her own car (a sporty blue convertible). She wrote newspaper columns and books, lectured, and taught, and the recognition and money meant a lot to her. By 1938, she was earning more than $60,000 a year (she donated most of it to charities that helped women). A White House usher recorded what Franklin and Eleanor did each day, and her list was usually three times as long as his.

Change and growth were her hallmarks. Roosevelt lost her fears, announcing, "I long ago reached the point where there is no living person whom I fear, and few challenges that I am not willing to face." Her early speeches were punctuated with panicky giggles, but she later became legendary for such soul-stirring statements as "No one can make you feel inferior without your consent" and "It's better to light a candle than to curse the darkness."

Independent women had once appalled her, and at first she vigorously opposed the idea of women voting. But her first book, *It's Up to the Women*, called for them to become more active in politics. She reminded Franklin that "women exist" when she saw his all-male lists for political appointments. A whole generation of women journalists got their start when she began holding weekly press conferences for women only; newspapers were then forced to hire women to get the story. Roosevelt exchanged several thousand letters with one reporter, Lorena Hickok; historians disagree about whether they were romantically involved.

A down-to-earth person who loved to put people at ease, Roosevelt cultivated an image of almost saintly serenity. "She gave off light," marveled a friend. Each morning, she either exercised in her room or rode her horse, Dot, with her male bodyguard (a former circus acrobat). She worked all day, hurried to change clothes for a formal dinner, and afterward returned to read and answer her beloved mail. Before bed she would walk the family dogs around the White House, admiring the view, then slip inside for a chat with Franklin. On New Year's Eve, she would work until ten minutes before midnight, join the family for a round of toasts, then dash back to her room to work a few more hours.

Some thought that always doing the right thing made Roosevelt too earnest, even boring. A wintry day would exhilarate her—but then she'd immediately fret about the homeless. Even choosing clothes involved duty—she wouldn't wear any she thought were products of unfair labor conditions. She wrote that hairdressers were a waste of time and was not a fashion plate, wearing sensible shoes, a big purse, bulky tweed suits, and hats adorned with flowers or red and green feathers. One Inauguration Day she was driven in an open car through a downpour and made an embarrassing entrance— "the dye in my hat had run down my face in a startling fashion."

There were plenty of people who despised Roosevelt—and they blitzed the White House with letters, urging that "the most dangerous woman in America" be muzzled. Cruel "Eleanor jokes" circulated, ridiculing her appearance and mannerisms. She was realistic about the hostility toward women in public life, and "one politician in the family is enough" was her standard reply to several invitations to run for office. She didn't believe that the public would be ready for a woman president anytime soon, but she was willing to indicate her support for male candidates she approved of—and it carried so much weight that they frequently sought it.

Roosevelt had no interest in cooking (another waste of time). She once served hot dogs to the king and queen of England. For other distinguished guests she would whip up eggs, scrambling them right at the table in a large silver dish, calling the menu for the evening "scrambled eggs with brains." Most of the time she depended on cooks, who often served plain dinners of boiled carrots and mutton.

She didn't know how to unwind. At his cocktail hour, Franklin insisted on gossip or talk about movies—such lightweight conversation was torture for Eleanor (plus she was a teetotaler). She did have a sense of humor (bursts of raucous laughter could be heard from her quarters), but she wasn't famous for it. When hurt or angry she would suffer silently rather than take action. She had a difficult time turning anybody down, and late in life wished she'd been more selective about her activities, especially when they took her away from home.

"I was certainly not an ideal mother," Roosevelt said. She did take her five children camping, arranged for sledding and skating, and took swimming lessons to conquer her fear of water so she could teach them to swim. But she later decided that fear had caused her to leave too much parenting to nurses and governesses, and that she'd been too strict. Neighbors once threatened to call the police when they saw her baby daughter strung up in a wire box near an open window—so strong was Roosevelt's belief in the value of fresh air. She treasured her relationships with her children as adults, and also with her twenty-three grandchildren and great-grandchildren.

"For over 40 years, I was only a visitor there," Roosevelt wrote about Hyde Park, the six-hundred-acre family farm. Franklin's mother was queen of the house, with its elegance and matching china; there was no special chair for Eleanor anywhere. A mile down the road, in a grove of pines, Franklin had a cottage called Val-Kill, and that became Eleanor's special place. Every chair was a different size (to make any person comfortable), none of the dishes matched, and frogs chorused her to sleep.

Franklin "might have been happier with a wife who was completely uncritical," she observed, but she persisted in hounding him, even after others could see that his health was failing. Nevertheless, he left most of his $2-million estate to her. She told reporters, "The story is over," but her activities grew more vigorous than ever. President Truman appointed her one of the first five American delegates to the United Nations, which she believed would be the world's best hope for peace.

Friends and family urged Roosevelt to slow down, but she continued to work sixteen-hour days, never took another vacation, and died at age seventy-eight, after a stroke.

Ever After

❧ By Franklin's second term the first lady was listed as one of the "Ten Most Powerful People in Washington." In the years since her death, many have ranked her as the most influential woman of all time.

❧ When Roosevelt noticed that just nine of President John Kennedy's first 240 appointments were women, she sent him a three-page list of qualified candidates. In response, he established the Commission on the Status of Women—a turning point in the American women's movement—and appointed her chair.

❧ "I am a die-hard Eleanor Roosevelt fan," Hillary Rodham Clinton said in 1995, speaking at the dedication of the Eleanor Roosevelt College at the University of California, San Diego. Clinton used her as evidence that a first lady can influence policy and remain popular, and even admitted to imaginary talks with her: "When confronted with a particular situation, I might say to Mrs. Roosevelt, 'Oh, my goodness, what do I do now?'"

Golda Meir

BORN IN KIEV, UKRAINE, 1898
DIED IN JERUSALEM, ISRAEL, 1978

Prime minister of Israel and one of the country's founders

GOLDA MEIR's earliest memory of her childhood in Russia was of her father nailing boards across the doors and windows. He was preparing for what was to come: Mobs trying to break in, screaming "Death to Jews!" She once said the explanation for her whole life was the desire to save other Jewish children from the terror and anger she'd felt.

After her family moved to the United States, Meir checked out stacks of books from the Milwaukee Public Library, got good grades (though report cards called her "talkative"), and thought about becoming a teacher. But her parents often kept her home to work in the family grocery store, and were so opposed to high school that they arranged for their fourteen-year-old daughter to marry a much older man.

Before that could happen, Meir crept out her window and journeyed by train to her married sister in Colorado. There she met Jews who believed that Jewish people had a right to a nation of their own. It was a seemingly impossible dream, in the face of enormous odds, but, starting in her teens, Meir dedicated herself to the cause.

Meir liked to flirt, and her childhood best friend said that "four out of every five boys we met fell in love with her." She chose Morris Meyerson, saying, "He isn't very handsome, but he has a beautiful soul." Neighbors smirked that she was the husband—she worked while he shopped, cleaned, cooked, and even bought her clothes.

Her happiest times were on a farm in Palestine, where men and women shared the land and duties equally. When she first arrived at the farm, she was even afraid of the chickens, but she was soon gathering eggs for everyone. She danced the hora late into every Friday night, and (when she needed money) took in laundry that she washed by hand.

Ever more single-minded about her cause, Meir separated from her husband and remained in Palestine (they never divorced, and stayed friends). She sometimes left her children, Sarah and Menachem, with other people while she traveled—conquering her guilt took "an almost superhuman effort of the will," but she believed she offered her children more by staying active in the world. Her greatest talent was for raising money for the new nation by giving speeches. After one visit to the United States, she came back with $50 million. Frequently described as being made of steel, she could inspire such emotion that "we always had to have our handkerchiefs ready," someone recalled.

She came close to "going to pieces" during the Holocaust, when Jews were systematically murdered. In 1948, she cried (as did many others) when she was one of the signers of Israel's Proclamation of Independence. Winning successive positions in the new government, she had enormous influence over every area of Israeli life, from education and employment to housing—and even where the bathrooms were located (inside instead of outside).

By the time Meir was elected prime minister of Israel, in 1969, she had more than forty-five years of political experience. Her advisers met in her kitchen at night, sitting around her green Formica table. Chain-smoking Chesterfields, thumping the table for order when needed, she would get up every so often to make sandwiches or more tea and coffee.

She trained herself to function on four hours of sleep. To get thinking time, she sometimes scrubbed her floor in the middle of the night. She relaxed by watching TV—with close friends she would imitate American commercials and laugh uncontrollably. Her home was full of African masks and statues (she traveled to Africa so often that many villages considered her their honorary queen). She usually wore sensible shoes and favored increasingly unstylish suits in black or gray. She had four or five bodyguards and was more afraid of blindness than of death—during times of danger she would cover her eyes.

Amid controversy over Israel's lack of preparation in the Yom Kippur War of 1973, Meir resigned. Her numerous health problems included cancer, which she kept secret for twelve years before she died at age eighty.

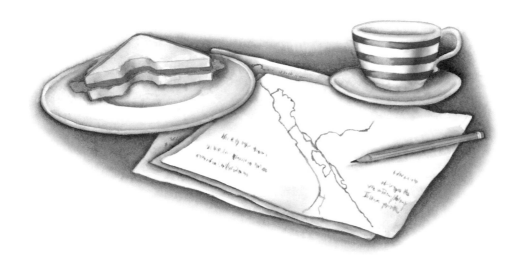

EVER AFTER

～ Reporters could never decide how to view Meir. One minute they would ask her about nuclear weapons (she always sought peace with her nation's neighbors, but insisted on Israel's right to defend itself), and then would ask about recipes (those cheese blintzes, that chicken soup). When she died, headlines around the world described her as "Israel's Uncrowned Queen," "Israel's Strongman," and "Israel's Intrepid Granny."

～ As one of the most influential women of the twentieth century, Meir was a heroine to the women's movement in the 1970s. A famous poster showed her taking the Israeli oath of office, with "But can she type?" as the ironic caption. Though Meir felt that "to be successful, a woman has to be much better at her job than a man," she was uncomfortable being a symbol. She worked in a "man's world" not to make a point but because that's where nations were built. The first time she saw the poster, Meir merely remarked, "You know, I never did learn to type."

Indira Gandhi

BORN IN ALLAHABAD, INDIA, 1917
DIED IN NEW DELHI, INDIA, 1984

Prime minister of India,
once one of the most popular leaders in the world

AS FAR BACK as she could remember, Indira Gandhi battled to free India from British rule. As a child she spied on police while pretending to play, gave "thunderous speeches" about freedom to servants, and threw her dolls onto a fire to protest goods made outside India. Mohandas Gandhi, the pacifist leader of the freedom movement, was a close family friend and her hero (but was not related).

Because of her rebellion against the British, she was even jailed—for more than a year, in grim conditions and plagued by white ants—along with her new husband, Feroze Gandhi, a lawyer who was also active in the fight. Avoiding the traditional Indian arranged marriage, Indira chose her husband and he came to live with her family. They had two sons, Rajiv and Sanjay, but later drifted apart and lived separately.

Well educated at various universities, Gandhi advised the first prime minister of the newly independent India (her father, Jawaharlal Nehru), then became minister of broadcasting, which was a key post in a mostly illiterate nation. Some assumed that this lone woman among the ministers—a "dumb doll"—could be easily manipulated. During her first speech, someone yelled, "She does not speak, she squeaks!" She did seem frail, even brittle, but soon won fame as a "tigress among one hundred monkeys."

Prime minister at age forty-eight, Gandhi struggled to unite a population of 720 million (with seven major religions, one thousand languages, and three thousand social divisions called castes). In every decision—limiting population growth, finding ways for women to participate in politics, sending India's first satellite into space, promoting the use of computers—she used one guideline: Is it good for the pride of the country?

"A Prime Minister must always be a little upset," she lamented. During her eighteen-hour workdays, hundreds of people crowded in to see her. She wore out her aides with her no-frills travel to distant villages, riding elephants when cars were unavailable. Her powerful position was frequently challenged by betrayals, customs that repressed women (she developed a thick skin), and violence. During one speech, a protester threw a rock and fractured her nose—she used her sari to cover the blood pouring down her face and finished the speech. She was not skilled at repartee, and used silence as one of her most intimidating weapons. Nervous gestures included rearranging the flowers in a vase, straightening the pictures on a wall, and an uncontrollable twitch in her right eye.

With so many plots against her, she stopped trusting most people. Many believed her son Sanjay encouraged Gandhi's most controversial decision: declaring a "state of emergency" when opponents seemed about to topple her. After she imprisoned them and censored the press, she was voted right out of office. But a few years later, in a spectacular comeback, she campaigned wearing garlands of onions, promising to lower the price of this vital ingredient in Indian cooking.

Every morning she chose carefully from her closet full of saris—her favorite was an old rose-colored one, but specific occasions required black or white, or mango, green, or yellow. Despite gossip about her handsome yoga instructor, she seemed to have no social life. She lived with her sons and took walks in their garden, which featured orchids, butterflies, tiger cubs, and a baby panda. She never learned to cook, but enjoyed her daughter-in-law Sonia's Italian specialties (it wasn't easy for her to find cooks she could trust not to poison her). At night she curled up in her favorite easy chair and watched videos, got back massages from a servant, played word games, and let all her grandchildren sleep in her room. Her secret dream was to be a writer, and one of her most thrilling memories was hearing Allen Ginsberg and other Beat poets read their work.

When she was sixty-six, Gandhi sent the army to drive Sikh terrorists out of a temple that was the holiest in the Sikh religion. Advisers cautioned her to remove Sikhs from her team of bodyguards, but she refused, not wanting to add to their humiliation. Later that year, as she walked through her garden, she was shot to death by two Sikh members of her security guard.

EVER AFTER

Within minutes of Gandhi's assassination, in 1984, riots broke out in New Delhi's streets. Four days later, four thousand Sikhs were dead, with twenty thousand injured. Gandhi's son Rajiv served as prime minister until 1991, when he, too, was murdered. In 1998, Gandhi's daughter-in-law, Sonia, emerged from seclusion to become a prominent figure in Indian politics.

"I do not regard myself as a woman but as a person with a job to do," Indira Gandhi insisted. But the imbalance of power angered her: "Women in India, perhaps in most of the world, are so dominated and discriminated against. There is so much unnecessary cruelty and humiliation." Her own power was of lasting significance for women in India (who traditionally entered their husbands' family as unpaid servants) and other poor countries.

Eva Perón

BORN IN LOS TOLDOS, ARGENTINA, 1919
DIED IN BUENOS AIRES, ARGENTINA, 1952

❧

*First lady of Argentina and
the most powerful woman in Latin America*

EVA PERÓN's one escape from her painful childhood was indulging in Hollywood fantasy—especially on Tuesdays, when three movies in a row cost just thirty cents. She made it through sixth grade, and at age fifteen (possibly with the help of a famous tango singer) got herself to the glittering big city of Buenos Aires.

There she took any role she could get in radio soap operas, movies, and the theater. Her reviews were not good, but no one tried harder to succeed. At a concert to benefit earthquake victims, she met the dashing Colonel Juan Perón, an equally ambitious army officer twice her age.

"She had guts," was his first reaction. One morning after he left for work, she rented a truck, delivered her possessions to Juan's apartment, and moved his current girlfriend out. When Juan returned for his siesta, he asked no questions, and he and Eva were never apart again. By the time he was elected president, she had gladly given up acting for marriage. A devout Catholic in most respects, she never had children and never spoke of it.

"I want to have a place in history," she said, and her husband gave her a platform. The thought of injustice always left her physically ill, almost unable to breathe. When she first began speaking out against injustices, she mispronounced words, but eventually she developed the poise of a lifelong public figure. Becoming a hypnotizing speaker, she could whip workers and the poor into a frenzy of devotion to "Evita." Women adored her after she got them the right to vote and legalized divorce. Her powerful role in a macho society caused some to loathe her, especially the military (who bitterly opposed her unsuccessful attempt to become vice president) and the wealthy. Enemies snickered that she was fat (she wasn't, though Juan didn't help by always nagging her to exercise).

One friend said Perón was part tiger, part dove. She spoke harshly and vulgarly to officials, but was scared to sleep alone. She never cried (her priest called her "the woman with no tears"), and liked to romp with Juan's many poodles. She took revenge on people who failed to treat her well, but also founded a charity that gave away millions. About the rich she said she could "bite them just as one crunches into a carrot or a radish," but she cared for the poor, even bathing lice-infested children.

"The poor like to see me beautiful," Perón said in defense of her world-famous wardrobe. Among the 283 rooms of the presidential palace (where she and Juan sometimes slid down the rail of the dramatic marble staircase for fun) were individual rooms for her hats, shoes, and jewels. To work she would often wear an elegant designer suit with a velvet collar. For formal occasions she brought out sequins, feathers, and her resplendent jewels—her favorite was an Argentine-flag brooch made of diamonds and sapphires (later sold for nearly $1 million). She had a nervous habit of nibbling on her jewelry (and one night ended up with green lips when her necklace

turned out to be made of painted noodles). She bleached her hair an unnatural, halo-like shade of gold.

Laden with diamonds, Perón rode to work in a Rolls-Royce (one of sixty-three cars she and Juan owned). But she didn't go home until everyone in line had been given a job, clothes, food, medicine (she wrote prescriptions herself), or simply money (she kept cash in her desk). She hugged and chatted, increasing the length of her day until she worked virtually around the clock. Always a dieter, as time went by she ate less and less.

Ignoring her health, she was diagnosed with cancer too late for doctors to do anything. A wire device held her upright during her last public appearance. Nearly hidden in a huge fur coat, she weighed less than eighty pounds. "I leave you my heart," she told her followers. To her maid, in her final hours, she said, "My mother would have married me to someone ordinary and I could never have stood it ... A decent woman has to get on in the world."

When she died, at age thirty-three, she was worth approximately $12 million.

EVER AFTER

An estimated three million people, lined up for miles, filed past Perón's casket. The crush killed at least eight and injured hundreds. Juan decided to preserve Eva's body forever and hired a pathologist who had perfected a technique using layers of special plastic. Fearful that her grave site would become a shrine, her enemies moved her corpse all over the world, inspiring bizarre legends. Yet when it returned to Argentina twenty-two years later to be displayed with Juan's, her body was so well preserved it looked as though she had just died.

"I will return, and I will be millions" were Perón's most famous words. But her many enemies undid much of her work after Juan—kept in power by his wife's popularity—was overthrown in 1955.

More than forty years after her death, her Cinderella story made it to Hollywood. The movie *Evita*, starring Madonna, was based on the Broadway musical of Eva Perón's life story.

Wilma Mankiller

BORN IN TAHLEQUAH, OKLAHOMA, 1945

᷎

Longtime American Indian leader and
chief of the Cherokee Nation for ten years

WILMA MANKILLER? The name inspired snickers during every roll call at school, and later lured the curious into halls to hear her speak. Mankiller is a Cherokee family name—an old military title for the one in charge of protecting a village. Although she does get tired of the jokes about it, Mankiller tries to stay good-humored and prefers to imply that she earned her name through her fierce deeds: "That usually shuts the person up."

Daughter of a full-blooded Cherokee father and a mother of Dutch and Irish descent, Mankiller spent her first ten years on a farm with no plumbing or electricity. She and her ten brothers and sisters walked three miles each way to school (at times without shoes), wore clothes made from scratchy flour sacks, hauled water from a spring, and survived by bartering with neighbors. She loved the sound of rain on their tin roof and exploring the surrounding forests—full of foxes, deer, mountain lions, and bobcats.

When her family moved to San Francisco during a government effort to relocate Indians from rural areas into large cities, Mankiller discovered TV, neon lights, elevators, toilets, bicycles, and signs in restaurants that said NO DOGS, NO INDIANS. City kids treated her as though she were from outer space—once she hit a teasing boy in the jaw so hard that he dropped to the ground. She ran away from home at least five times.

She made it through high school (with grades ranging from A to F), did some clerical work (punching one boss who got too chummy during a Christmas party), and married at age seventeen.

"I was a typical housewife at that time," Mankiller said. She raised two daughters, Felicia and Gina, and taught them to share her love of reading, develop a sense of humor, and dance all around the house. In 1969, her life changed forever when a group of students occupied Alcatraz Island to call attention to five centuries of inhumane treatment of Indians. Awakened to injustice, she began developing programs to help tribes, and graduated from college with the encouragement of a woman who saw her leadership potential. Her wealthy Ecuadoran husband disapproved of her new activities, especially when she bought a little red car without his permission so she could get to events on her own. Her second husband, Charlie Soap, is a full-blooded Cherokee and a renowned dancer at powwows; he puts Mankiller at the top of his "heroes list."

Mankiller worked her way up through the Cherokee hierarchy to the top, becoming, in 1987, the first woman elected principal chief of a tribe. She ruled over a population of 140,000, with an annual budget of $75 million and 1,200 employees. Her young grandson thought it cool that "grandma was the chief."

Mankiller found it shocking to be resented just because she was a woman. Protesters slashed her car tires, made death threats, said hurtful things. She called her wittiest friend and asked for some funny replies she could make. One man interrupted her so obnoxiously throughout a meeting that, before the next one, she arranged to have control of the microphones: When "this very same fellow started giving me a hard time, I just cut off his microphone."

Eventually, she decided that leadership had so little to do with gender that all she could do was carry on with her work, despite opposition. Mankiller was legendary for her exuberant optimism, even in the face of almost overwhelming problems: "I believe in the old Cherokee injunction to 'be of a good mind.' Today it's called positive thinking." She strongly encouraged young people to enter public service, take risks, and "dance along the edge of the roof."

Along with her political struggles, Mankiller has battled ill health. She was once almost killed (in a freak car accident in which her best friend died), and endured seventeen operations afterward. Fighting cancer, plus a chronic muscle disease, she has required two kidney transplants (eight of her relatives offered theirs). In 1995, her health caused her to step down as chief.

EVER AFTER

As a fighter for Indian rights, Mankiller said, "I want to be remembered as the person who helped us restore faith in ourselves." Part of the fight was against stereotypes: "If I see one more book with a native person standing on top of a hill with hands towards the sky, I think I'm going to throw up." She has ended speeches by saying, "I hope my spending a little time with you will help to erase any stereotypes you might have had about what an Indian chief looks like."

Mankiller also considers herself an advocate for women, and predicted that more women will take on leadership roles in society: "Prior to my election, young Cherokee girls would never have thought that they might grow up and become chief." She claimed the hardest thing she ever did was to stand up at her first meeting and say, "I disagree . . . There's a better way." *Ms.* magazine named her Woman of the Year in 1987.

Aung San Suu Kyi

ॐ

Revolutionary leader in Burma (Myanmar),
general secretary of the National League for Democracy

THOUGH AUNG SAN SUU KYI was just a baby when her father, Aung San, was assassinated, she never stopped thinking about him. Burma's greatest hero, Aung San led the struggle for independence from Britain in the 1940s. After his death a brutal military government grabbed power. Suu Kyi was educated mostly abroad (reading detective stories between studies). After she graduated from Oxford University in England, she worked for the United Nations, in New York.

Then she settled into a quiet life as the wife of a British professor, becoming an excellent cook and the giver of perfect birthday parties for Kim and Alexander, her sons. In 1988, she went to Burma to help her ailing mother. Her mother died after a few months—and by then Suu Kyi had given her most famous speech. In front of the diamond-encrusted Shwedagon Pagoda, Burma's most sacred shrine, half a million people heard this British housewife's passionate call for peaceful change. "As my father's daughter, I felt I had a duty to get involved," she said later.

Suu Kyi remained in Burma and continued to speak out, with a fearlessness that became legendary. One day she calmly confronted army troops aiming their rifles at her, ready to carry out their orders to shoot. She walked on toward them, and not until the last possible moment did a commander step in and order the rifles lowered.

The National League for Democracy, which she helped establish, won the next election with eighty-two percent of the vote. The government refused to honor the election, and shot thousands of unarmed protesters. Soldiers surrounded Suu Kyi's two-story house. They cut the phone wires, blocked her lake view with barbed wire, installed fifteen armed guards around the clock, and shut down her contact with followers, family, and media.

Agonizing that her supporters were tortured and jailed under far more appalling conditions than hers, she tried to keep sane with routine: She rose at 4:30 A.M. for exercise and meditation (she is a devout Buddhist), then read biographies or philosophy,

played piano or guitar, and listened to the radio. When she ran out of money, she sold off the furniture; her house grew bare, its crumbling walls black with mildew. Some days she was too weak, from hunger, to get out of bed. Her hair fell out, her weight dropped to ninety pounds, her garden of scented flowers grew dense with weeds and squirmy with snakes. Thinking of the sons she had left in England made her cry.

She could have surrendered at any time—if she agreed to leave Burma forever. Instead, she thought of herself as a splinter of glass, "with its sharp, glinting power to defend itself against hands that try to crush." Her husband, Michael Aris, said, "There was never any point in my trying to convince Suu to do anything but what she had decided to do."

Six difficult years later, pressure from the outside world ended her house arrest. Then, each weekend, supporters lifted amplifiers into the trees around her home, and she climbed onto a desk to address the crowds. She always ended by warning everyone to go home quickly, and remained outside until she was sure no one had been arrested. When crowds at her blue gates grew to five thousand—students, monks in saffron vestments, nuns in pink robes—the government banned her speeches.

"I look upon myself as a politician," says Suu Kyi, "and that's not a dirty word, you know." She wears lungyi, the Burmese sarong, and three kinds of flowers in her hair, petals often falling on her shoulders during her twelve-hour workday as she continues her fight for a democratic government. She exchanges news with visitors over rice, green tea, and giggles. A friend says, "You have to realize Suu is really funny."

Still Burma's hope for freedom, Suu Kyi remains in her house. She is free to escape to another country, but says, "You will have to take me to the airport in chains, because otherwise I will never leave."

EVER AFTER

 Suu Kyi was awarded the 1991 Nobel Peace Prize for her extraordinary courage. The first person to receive it while in captivity, she was represented at the ceremony by her husband and sons. A photograph of her faced the audience. With her $1.3 million prize money, she established a health-and-education fund for the Burmese, especially benefiting minorities and refugees.

 Suu Kyi's house is Burma's most visited attraction. The government spies on her with hidden cameras and tapped phones, and she is unable to travel without harassment. As the daughter of the national hero, she is theoretically immune from harm, but in fact her life is always in danger.

Rigoberta Menchú

❧

*Guatemalan leader who drew the
world's attention to native Indian rights*

THE FIRST TIME she spoke in public, she was so nervous that she literally forgot her own name—Rigoberta Menchú. But starting in her teens, she spoke up anyway, to help Guatemala's Indian peasants resist massive military oppression, and then (when she fled the country to save her life) to educate the rest of the world. Telling her story and others' over and over, traveling from place to place, sleeping in a different house every night—this was her way of triumphing over a childhood of horrifying violence and misery.

One of nine children in a Quiché Mayan family, she grew up in a village of both pure beauty and grinding poverty, in a misty rainforest. Small children worked every daylight hour on nearby coffee and cotton plantations, and most, suffering from malnutrition, didn't live past age fifteen. Menchú slept in the clothes she worked in all day, always had stomach worms, and at age twelve found a job as a maid in the city, where the dogs had better food than she did. Like other Indians, she had no rights of citizenship and was vulnerable to abuse. One of her few pleasures was to spend time with women looking among the stones in the river for snails to sell. When soldiers began harming her friends, Menchú's political activism caught fire and she left the village for good.

Indians disappeared by the thousands during Guatemala's civil war. The army arrested and tortured much of Menchú's family, and murdered so many of her relatives that she considered herself an orphan: "I couldn't bear to be the only one left. I actually wanted to die." Narrowly escaping capture several times, she used her anger and hatred to fuel a search for justice rather than for revenge, saying, "Life was painful but new times are coming... The solution is energy, work, convictions, and giving of yourself, with enthusiasm."

For years Menchú was a nobody, struggling to draw attention to Guatemala's Indians. Between speaking tours organized by a growing number of supporters, she hung around the United Nations building in New York, dashing from meeting to meeting, pestering people, learning the names of employees and guards. Her goal was to be "like a drop of water on a rock. After drip, drip, dripping in the same place, I begin to leave a mark." Friends persuaded her to turn her dramatic life story into a book: *I, Rigoberta Menchú*. The numbing experiences she described, representing those of "poor people throughout the world," made her internationally famous at age twenty-three.

Her attempts to return to Guatemala were thwarted by death threats—once she was met at the airport by four hundred police officers ready to arrest her. In other countries, suspicious border agents often stopped her, as though being poor and Indian were a crime. Then, in 1992, she won the Nobel Peace Prize for her work. Whenever officials thoroughly searched her belongings (a few family keepsakes and a laptop computer), she

would delight in telling them about her award, lecturing them on racism, even calling a press conference to publicize the mistreatment.

Menchú also encountered trouble from fellow rebels who resented being led by an Indian woman. She found it "very difficult" to give orders to men, but insisted that women and men fight as equals. Her response to intimidation and harassment was, "That is not my problem—I'm not going to step aside." For years, she thought marriage would be incompatible with her work (and she didn't want to risk losing another family). In time, she wed Angel Canil, a fellow revolutionary who was always encouraging her. They have one son, Mash.

"Wearing many colors gives me life," says Menchú. She wears traditional Guatemalan multicolored dresses with rich embroidery, bright sashes and scarves, and necklaces of silver coins and red beads. In private, she is gentle, reserved, and graceful (which she credits to learning how to pick coffee berries without damaging branches). Every morning she cooks tortillas, perfectly round and as thin as paper, with black beans and hot peppers. To relax she makes necklaces, crochets, or writes poetry.

As a high-profile human rights activist, Menchú has ever-present bodyguards. But she seldom passes a night without waking in panic from a dream that the Guatemalan army has come for her. "They can kill me at any time," she says, "but let it be when I'm fulfilling a mission, so I'll know that my blood will not be shed in vain."

EVER AFTER

For being a "shining individual example of people who manage to preserve their humanity in brutal and violent surroundings," Menchú became the youngest person (at age thirty-three) and the first Indian ever to receive the Nobel Peace Prize. Her first public words after hearing the news were, "How I would love to have all my family alive and here with me! Because life is peace. I desire life and peace." The prize was controversial, and some charged that Menchú's protests have not always been peaceful. She maintained that her methods were political, not violent. "If I had chosen the armed struggle, I would be in the mountains now"—with the other armed fighters.

Menchú thought of her autobiography as a tool to raise people's awareness. It has been translated into at least a dozen languages and is read in universities around the world. In 1998, published reports claimed that she exaggerated some of her experiences. A neighbor from her village said, "The truth may be distinct from how she has told it, but that does not mean Rigoberta did not suffer greatly in those years." Menchú, dismissing the claims as a racist agenda intended to discredit her, said she would "defend the book to the death."

Guatemala's civil war ended in 1996, after thirty-six years of strife. Menchú continues to speak out for social justice in cases of human rights abuse around the world. With her $1.2 million Nobel Prize money, she set up a foundation to fund projects that contribute to "the urgent need for change in our society," particularly to gain rights for native Indian people, women, children, and refugees.

For Further Reading

Of the many resources consulted for this book, these are some of the most useful.

De Madariaga, Isabel. *Catherine the Great: A Short History*. New Haven, Conn.: Yale Univ. Press, 1990.

Dujovne Ortiz, Alicia. *Eva Perón*. Translated by Shawn Fields. New York: St. Martin's Press, 1996.

Erickson, Carolly. *Her Little Majesty: The Life of Queen Victoria*. New York: Simon & Schuster, 1997.

————. *To the Scaffold: The Life of Marie Antoinette*. New York: William Morrow, 1991.

Flamarion, Edith. *Cleopatra: The Life and Death of a Pharaoh*. Translated by Alexandra Bonfante-Warren. New York: Harry N. Abrams, 1997.

Fraser, Antonia. *The Warrior Queens*. New York: Alfred A. Knopf, 1989.

Freedman, Russell. *Eleanor Roosevelt: A Life of Discovery*. New York: Clarion Books, 1993.

Gies, Frances. *Joan of Arc: The Legend and the Reality*. New York: Harper & Row, 1981.

Jayakar, Pupul. *Indira Gandhi: An Intimate Biography*. New York: Pantheon, 1992.

Mankiller, Wilma, and Michael Wallis. *Mankiller: A Chief and Her People*. New York: St. Martin's Press, 1993.

Martin, Ralph G. *Golda Meir: The Romantic Years*. New York: Charles Scribner's Sons, 1988.

Menchú, Rigoberta. *Crossing Borders*. Translated and edited by Ann Wright. New York: Verso Books, 1998.

O'Brien, Mary Barmeyer. *Jeannette Rankin: Bright Star in the Big Sky*. Helena, Mont.: Falcon, 1995.

Rubin, Nancy. *Isabella of Castille: The First Renaissance Queen*. New York: St. Martin's Press, 1991.

Seagrave, Sterling, with Peggy Seagrave. *Dragon Lady: The Life and Legend of the Last Empress of China*. New York: Alfred A. Knopf, 1992.

Seward, Desmond. *Eleanor of Aquitaine: The Mother Queen*. New York: Dorset Press, 1978.

Taylor, Marian. *Harriet Tubman*. New York: Chelsea House, 1991.

Victor, Barbara. *The Lady: Aung San Suu Kyi, Nobel Laureate and Burma's Prisoner*. Boston: Faber & Faber, 1998.

Wallach, Janet. *Desert Queen: The Extraordinary Life of Gertrude Bell, Adventurer, Adviser to Kings, Ally of Lawrence of Arabia*. New York: Nan A. Talese/Doubleday, 1996.

Weir, Alison. *The Life of Elizabeth I*. New York: Ballantine Books, 1998.